The Art of Writing and Publishing on Amazon

Ibrahim O. Arasi

CONTENTS

FAILURE OR SUCCESS? WHO DETERMINES THAT?

Are you a failing writer? Who decides your status as a failure? Is it your results? Is it your colleagues? Is it your friends or your circumstances? Nothing and no one but you, batch you a failure.

1. In spite of failures, hardship, disappointment, a man who is determined to succeed will never give up on his dreams

2. To be successful in whatever you do, don't ever stop growing your

dream- keep pushing your dream, and keep working on your dreams.

HOW DO YOU WORK ON YOUR DREAM AS A WRITER?

1. Spend Time By Yourself

Don't try to be other people. Be yourself; discover you and not other person. Work on the "you" that you have discovered.

Be close to you, groom you, be familiar with you and get the counterfeit, the losers and the alternatives out of your life.

Please Note: If you stay a copycat, you can never be an original

Always remember that you are a dreamer, you are uncommon, a special breed and your standard is high.

2. Invest In You

Invest in your mind, in your dream, in your passion- groom your dream, get knowledge. Go for Conferences, read books, go for further training and don't let anybody steal your dream

3. Don't Give Up Until You Get It

No matter the outcome of your efforts. Be it failure, errors, mistakes or outright rejection. Say to yourself it is not over until you win.

QUALITIES OF A WINNING WRITER

1. Focus

To stay focus is to keep at a thing despite so many alternatives at one's disposal. Stay focused on your passion; be determined to keep at it until you achieve it. Keep your eyes single on the mark and stay on your lane till you get to the finish line.

2. Tenacity

A winner must learn to keep at it. Keep doing the same thing with the same vigor and positivity. The ability to stay on with your vision without letting out its steam is called tenacity.

3. Doggedness

It is a common saying that quitters never win and winners never quit. And that's it. You must remain resilient, relentless and stubborn with your vision and dream if you want to see success at the end of the tunnel.

4. Investment In Your Self Mentality

Have you seen a man that is confident, bold and succeeding in his endeavors? You can look out for a man that is constantly adding knowledge to knowledge. That is a man sourcing for relevant information, a man upgrading himself constantly to meet the challenges of this age.

5. Give All That It Will Take

Your vision or passion deserves your best. Give it everything you've got and everything it takes. Empty yourself into your vision and see the results thereafter.

6. Collaboration

One person will achieve for one and two people will achieve for two. If you want to make a global impact with your vision, work with a team, a group or a people. Everyone has his part to play, no man has the capacity to do the job of every other person.

7. Relationship

Nurture your relationships; invest in it, care for it, value it, cherish it, uphold and keep your relationships. You need people as you journey on in life and how you handle them will determine how responsive they'll be to you when the need arises.

8. Knowledge And Upgraded Knowledge

You must learn to update yourself with relevant information. What solve today's problem may not be able to solve tomorrow problem.

9. Getting The Right Skill

Empower your vision/writing with the right skills. This will in no small measure make work easy and the journey (journey of success) faster.

10. Patience To See Result

Patience simply means, give it time. Give your vision/writing time, give yourself time to develop, to emerge, to evolve. Patience is a virtue and it is worth emulating.

THE MYSTERY IN WRITING AND STRONG WRITING

THE MYSTERY IN WRITING

Have you ever imagined how a writer is prompted to write or what makes a writer write? This is exactly the mystery in writing. To know about the mystery in writing, consider and understand the following salient points about writing:

1. Writing is not restricted to a set of people, race, language or color. Anyone can choose to write and become a billionaire earning in dollars and pounds through this skill.

2. Writing goes farther than where the two legs of the writer could possibly get to. So, through your writing, your message(s) can get to the ends of the earth making a global impact.

3. Your writing can create a huge traffic of followers for you round the globe thereby having more people believing in your cause and convictions.

4. Your book(s) makes you an authority and a voice wherever you find yourself.

5. A Book is a legacy that outlive you the writer. It also and always serve as a blessing to it readers. It also proffers solutions to gener-

ations all over the universe long after your death.

6. Through your books, your generations to come can be partakers of the royalties that accrue from the sales of your books.

7. Through your books, you can become famous, powerful and highly influential.

8. You can also enjoy other channels of blessings via other opportunities accessible through your books. Such opportunities can turn out to be mega breakthroughs that will permanently change your all round status.

Writing is the act of scribbling something on paper—it could be your thoughts, expressions, ideas etc. It is the process of using symbols such as letters of the alphabets, punctuation and spaces to communicate expressions, ideas and thoughts in a readable form.

I know you might have some questions in your mind "Why are some books selling more than the others?" Why are some authors making impact than the others?

Why is it that some books sold just few copies whereas others sell millions of copies? What are the reasons? The reasons are not far-fetched. It is because of the type of writing. And that brings us to what we know as strong writing.

WHAT IS A STRONG WRITING?

This is a writing that is captivating right from start. It is a writing that captures the attention of the reader as a result of the style, language, imagery and rhetorics employed right from start and hold him bound until he finished reading the whole book. Such books stir up the curiosity of the reader and keep him yearning for more until the very end of the story line.

In another definition, a strong writing is one that meets the needs of your targeted audience, to the extent that they would be willing to pay for it or do anything to have your work.

This simply means that a book should be targeted to solve a problem. People pay very high price for the knowledge they need to have their problems solved.

POINTS TO NOTE FOR STRONG WRITING

1. Your Passion

Your writing should be in line with your passion. It should be about something you are an authority in. An area you have so much information and so much grace. Your subject of writing should be so convincing, so real such that it will always impact the targeted world.

2. Your Audience

Every subject has an audience. It's important you know your audience, know their language, know how to access them and also know the kind of bait they will be attracted to, you should be able to know and decode what they want, from what they need as well as what they strongly desire.

You should also be familiar with the solution they are looking for. It is important you tailor your book along those lines of thoughts; after all, the subject matter of your writing is not about yourself but your audience.

3. The Market Gap

Know your market! Know the trend in the different kinds of markets especially in the post Covid world- that includes the Market Space- Global or Local. Pay attention to the "The Problem - Solution gap!"

Watch out and proffer solutions to all of these areas. Income will naturally follow when these raised points are addressed. There is no two ways about it. As long as you are solving a problem, money will come.

INTRODUCTION TO E-BOOK CREATION AND PUBLICATION

INTRODUCTION TO EBOOK

We live in the age of electronic EVERYTHING: E-commerce, E-banking, E-tickets, E-gift-cards, E-cigarettes, and the list go on.

Why?

This is simply because people love the idea of doing everything from virtually anywhere on any device. With that being said, it's no surprise that we've started revolutionizing the way we do just about EVERYTHING.

What started as a way to make everyday activities easier has made its way to our leisure activities: reading being one that comes to mind right away. We've introduced Ebooks as a way of making pastimes enjoyable and flexible.

SO, WHAT'S AN E-BOOK?

An E-Book is an electronic book, also known as E-Book or eBook. E-Book is a book of publication made available in digital form, consisting of text, images, or both, readable on the flat-panel display of computers or other electronic devices.

It can also be defined thus: A text presented in a format which allows it to be read on a computer or handheld device.

Many titles which are available in printed versions can be read as ebooks, including best selling fictions, classics, and reference texts.
Please Note: In creating your E-Book, you start from the process of using Microsoft Word to format your document.

So, let's consider the things you'll need to know and of in having a great manuscript for your E-Book.

1. Cover Page

2. Dedication

3. Acknowledgments

4. Table of Contents (TOC)

5. Copyright

6. Introduction

7. Body/Chapters/Interior

8. Blurb

9. About The Author

So we are going to run through them as fast as possible. These are what we are already familiar with but we are here to shed more light on them.

Cover Page

That's the first thing you see or come across in a book. A cover page must be catchy, classy, and attractive (depending on your audience or industry you're writing for).There is a saying that you don't judge a book by its cover.

That's does not apply here. Sometimes, in fact most times, people get attracted to a book with the kind of front cover it has.

There is another saying that the first impression matters. But in the case of picking a cover page, (front cover), have this in mind: FRONT impression matters.
So, to create your cover. The following are the processes and things you need.

1. A customized image, like the one you created or use/get any image of your choice.

2. An author's image ready

3. A concise "About the book" ready in MS Word

4. A concise "About the Author" ready in MS Word

There are 2 types of images you can use for your cover designs

a. The images on the Amazon gallery

b. Your own images.

You can decide which to use.

For the images on the Amazon gallery, you don't have copyright issues in using them. But for others, be sure of permission.

Don't worry, during the practical class of practicing what you have learnt in this book, you will get to see all of this.

Dedication

A book's dedication is a way for authors to bestow a high honor on a person (or small group of people) they want to praise or otherwise spotlight. That is somebody that has affected their life positively, in one way or the other.

We must try as much as possible to ensure that this shouldn't be more than a page. It is better that way.

Acknowledgments

The Acknowledgements section is where you recognize and thank everyone who helped you with your book. The editors, the proofreaders, the typist, contributors, advisers, spouse, children etc

It's a way to display your appreciation to them in a public and permanent forum.

Like I said about our Dedication, let's try to also make our acknowledgement to be as short as possible.

There are some authors who would want to thank the whole world in their acknowledgement.
Funny enough, not many people go through your acknowledgements. They just skip it and go straight to the next page. But if it is short enough, they probably may.

But if it will be too long, maybe 1 and a half pages, or 2 pages are enough.

Well it's all a matter of choice, there is no hard and fast rule on writing acknowledgements

Table Of Contents (Toc)

The table of contents (TOC) is the roadmap to each portion of your writing. It allows readers to locate specific information or revisit their favorite parts within the text. It entails the different chapters/parts of a book. It is a quick guide for people to leap to a particular chapter.

Copyright

This is the protection ownership rights to the contents of the book. It is a legal means of protecting an author's work. It is a type of intellectual property that provides exclusive publication, distribution, and usage rights for the author.

In simpler terms, copyright is the right to copy. This means that the original creators of products and anyone they give authorization to are the only ones with the exclusive right to reproduce the work.

Of course we all must have heard the word "Piracy". It is a huge crime. Piracy refers to the unauthorized duplication of copyrighted content.

Introduction

Several things attract and make people buy your books. One of such is the introduction, beside the cover design, blurb et cetera .

Please Note:
The best time to write your introduction, isn't before you create the interior, rather it comes after you have written the whole book.
This is because it is meant to tell readers in summary what to expect from the book

So writing your introduction before finishing your book interior or content may not convey the right message.

You must have finished your book before you write your introduction because it gives an insight into what the book is all about.

Body/Chapter/Interior

Here is where you start your story. It is where you convey whatever you wish to tell and inform about the whole gist.

The body of your book or chapters or interior is where you start your story or whatever you wish to convey and the whole concept/gist. This is where you break your ideas or story down in bit and pieces for your readers to follow.

The body of your writing is also known as the main content. It contains the purpose of your write up.

In writing the body of your book otherwise known as the content or the main message or idea, there is the need to be orderly, systematic, employing the use of clear and simple language and expression.

It is also the detailed part of your book. You can express your thoughts with the use of graphics, photos to further illustrate your ideas

If your body does not pass a message. Then you have wasted all your efforts and time...

Even if your cover page is attractive, and your content is not interesting or is lacking materials, it your book will not make sense in the long run. Remember the saying that ends justify the means.

Blurb

The blurb is that short description of your book, written behind or at the back of your book.

This is similar to or can also be referred to as the "ABOUT THE

BOOK".

Although a professional/standard book does not have that title "ABOUT THE BOOK", like abstracts or magazines. You just go ahead and write the description. Take note of your audience and industry to know the appropriate language to use!

About The Author

Last but not the least is ABOUT THE AUTHOR which is a short description about you and should be written in the "third person" format.
Writing in third person is writing from the third-person point of view, or outsider looking in, and it uses pronouns like he, she, it, or they. It differs from the first person, which uses pronouns such as I and me, and from the second person, which
uses pronouns such as you and yours.

FORMATTING: THE BASIC METHOD

THE KNOW-HOW OF FORMATTING

L et us consider how you can format your manuscript to fit into Amazon platform book platform.

There are steps and ways we will be considering in order to format your work into other presentable and acceptable forms publishable on the Amazon site.

THE BASICS OF E-BOOK PUBLISHING

We are going to focus more on the first important: Formatting your materials for your E-Book publishing...

What Formatting Is

Formatting is the layout of your documents in a presentable manner that will be able to pass on the Amazon platform.

Please Note: You cannot write your materials anyhow or put your manuscript the way you like because Amazon platform will not allow it.

There is a profession way, a global standard of writing your manuscript, and that is what is expected of you.

Good news: The good news is that if you know the secrets of publishing books on Amazon, it will like bread and butter.

But, before that can happen, you must pay the price to know it and be diligent to apply yourself to the new truth.

Formatting guides you in building your book in preparation your eBook Creation and Publishing.
There are 10 steps you need to take to format your manuscript. They include:

1. Set your page and margin

2. Choose suitable styles and customize same.

3. Format the interiors- Chapters

4. Fix your cover designate

5. Pagination

6. Headers fixation

7. Extras

8. Add images if available

9. Table of Content (TOC)

10. Proofread and convert to PDF

If you are able to follow these steps, you are good to go. I mean

If you carefully follow the abovementioned steps, your E-Book is on the way to be published.

The good news is that all these steps can be achieved with Microsoft Word Software. The most used trim size is 6" x 9".

Talking about Publishing on Amazon, it can either be E-Book (Digital Publication) or Paperback Publication.

Another good news is that you can have your book published on the two platforms, which can go live in two days once it is approved.

Paperback

A paperback also known as a softcover of softback is a type of book characterized by a thick paper or paperboard cover, and often held together with glue rather than stitches or staples.

Paperbacks editors of books are issued when a publisher decides to release a book in a low-cost format.

So, it's your hardcopy version of your book, while the digital publication is the softcopy of the same book.

However, it is easier to go through the Amazing Amazon App to get your softcopy unless than 3 days (with all the support features from the application), and then proceed to produce same as hardcopy which turn out to be very cheap, economical and quality based process.

All you need to do is fill the form after which you will be allocated ISBN IMMEDIATELY, and you then proceed to prepare your cover page. You have a variety of range to choose from. You can use the same cover for your paper back.

Just imagine, getting a printer to produce 500copies of a 300page book for N1.5million, then try to
produce a sof copy of the same book on Amazon in less than three days, and your book is up on Amazon for FREE. And your book is still producing or printing money for you. Amazing!

The good news is that you can earn for life as Amazon will do the Print for you. Yoy don't need to go to local printers to print for you again.

Now, understand the basics, that's the difference between manual labour and digital work space.

May I ask you which will you prefer between manual printing and digital book printing? Which one is more cost effective for authors like you?

HOW TO CREATE YOUR COVER

So, to create your cover, the following are the process and things you need:

1. A customized image, like the one you created or use/get any image of your choice.

2. An author's image ready

3. A concise About The Book ready in MS Word

4. A concise About The Author ready for n MS Word

There are 2 types of images you can use for your cover designs.
1. The images on the Amazon gallery

2. Your own Images

You can decide which to use.

For the images on the Amazon gallery, you don't have copyright issues in using them. But for others, be sure of permission.

Now, we are going full time PRACTICAL. Time for you to switch on your system (Laptop or Desktop) is now.

There is a ready-made App/Software made specially for you to be able to easily use to create and format your manuscript. This App/Software is called The Create Space Formatte. You are to download it in your system and save it under Document.

Just imagine getting a publisher to produce 400 copies of a 200 pages book for N1.6m. And then, you now produce a soft copy of the same book on Amazon in less than 3 days for a Zero naira. I mean in less than three days, you are already an author and your book is up for sale on Amazon for Free. All of these right from the comfort of your home. Wow! Honestly, which will you prefer?

Now, understand the basics, that's the difference between manual labour and digital workspace.

The manual way is no doubt no bad in creating and publishing your book but I bet you'll opt in for the digital publication style since it's what you would rather do now since we are in the digital age.

But it's just better you know how to yourself rather than take your works to a publisher who may not give you the best you want.

Once you know how to create, format and publish your books yourself on the Amazon site by the good technical know-how of all it take to publish on it, you're sure to publish your works at the speed of light.

Good News

The good news is that you can earn for life on Amazon. Amazon will do the print for you, Amazon will publish for you and Amazon will sell your eBook and paperback for you.

You don't need to go to local printers to print for you again, not any more. Remember: digital book is the future.

FORMATTING: THE ADVANCED METHOD

In the previous chapter, we consider the formatting of our works and manuscripts using the made Create Space Formatte template.

The Create Space Format template enables us to easily format our written works by copying and pasting them from MS Word. The template is good and useful in making our works easy to format into acceptable and publishable format on the Amazon platform.

However, we discovered that it is quite tedious and stressful. Besides, it doesn't allow some space to input some other necessary features as found in some books such as Preface, Foreword, et cetera. Therefore, needs call for the improvement on the Format template.

As a result, Amazon came up with a more advanced and better software called Kindle Create App. This software was specially designed to take care of the lapses and disadvantages of the initial Create Space App which though also useful, but not as effective and easier to use like the Kindle Create App.

USING THE KINDLE CREATE APP TO FORMAT

It is imperative that you know and master the art of using the Kindle Create App to format your manuscripts and create beautiful and lovely books ready for publication on your KDP Amazon page.

The Masters Class Training is the Crux of the training exercise. It is rightly termed by the boss himself as the SENSE AND ESSENCE of the training. Without mastering the use of the advanced App, that is, the Kindle Create App, you have merely wasted your time and efforts.

This is because it is the main reason you have enrolled for the Masters Class Training which you
paid for, although the money you paid is quite incomparable to the values you learned and earned for yourself.

And this can be doubled up and increased after you are able to master the use of the App as taught by the head coach himself, Ogapatapata.

With the Kindle Create App, you'll be able to prepare a well, ready-made formatted, publishable and acceptable manuscript on the KDP Amazon site.

You'll also be able to create beautiful interior by starting with an unformatted manuscript which you're going to start work with. And finish it up into a ready file just the way you want it to appear and get published.

When you open your kindle Create App on your laptop/desktop, you'll see two options at the left bottom corner. The options are:

1. Open an Existing File

2. Choose

Since you are using it for the first time, you'll go to the Choose option and click it.

Please Note:

If you have started using the Kindle Create Appto create and design manuscripts before, it is Open an Existing Option you'll chose, or you just click the particular file which you want to work on because it would have been saved as you work and save by clicking and saving it using the save button at the top left hand corner of your manuscript you are working on.

On choosing the Choose Menu, you'll select manuscript file you want to work on and click open. After this, the Kindle Create App automatically uploads and imports you're the file/manuscript.

Please Note Again:

It takes a while for the file to be uploaded and prepared for formatting on the Kindle Create App. You'll notice this as the Kindle Create App prepares your file by a "little time" preparation. All you need to do at this stage is to exercise some patience.

If at this stage you remember that the uploading file is not what you want to work on, you can choose to stop the uploading/importing by clicking cancel. But why do that when you can leave it to complete the uploading/importing and save that file for a later work, and choose the file you want to work on again for the Kindle Create App to prepare and import it.

Once it shows import successful, you'll click the Get Started menu to start working on your book to be formatted and published. If your book has been well formatted during the Kindle Create App import, it will give you a table of content which you could accept or reject.

There is something you need to know about every file you want to format into a beautifulbook with the Kindle Create App. At the top left Corner, you'll see the Front Matter which has a + menu in front of it.

The Front Matter has the following:

* Title Page

* Copyright

* Dedication

* Epigraph

*Table of Contents (TOC)

*Preface

*Introduction

*Prologue

*Foreword
*Standard Page (Front Matter)

All the above has to do with selecting to use for your books to be created and formatted provided you have them or want to use them in your book. What you'll just do is click them in turn to fill the information at the required page after clicking them.

For Example, after you click the title page, it'll display the following for you to fill.

*Book Title (REQUIRED)

*Book Subtitle

*Author Name

*Publisher

*Publisher Logo

*Select Image

*Create Page

*Cancel

Also, for the Copyright Page section, it will show the following for you to fill after clicking it:

*Copyright Owner (REQUIRED) (This is you, i.e your name)

*Year of Publication (REQUIRED)

*Rights (REQUIRED) (You will need to edit the information here by changing and inputting the ISBN Number there into your own given/assigned ISBN Number of your book by Amazon.) I believe you have been taught how to generate ISBN Number for your book. You can then click the Create Page after you are done.

Below the Front Matter is the Back Matter. On clicking the + menu in front of it, you'll see:

*Books By This Author

*About The Author

*Books in This Series
*Praise For The Author

*Epilogue
*Afterword

*Acknowledgements

*Standard Page

Let me quickly illustrate by using Books By This Author and About The Author.

If you click Books By This Author, the following are what will be required of you to submit:

*Number of Books (You'll choose the number)

*Book Title

*Amazon Store Link

*Description

*Create Page

*Cancel

You'll click Create Page after filling the information or choose to cancel.

If you click About The Author, you'll be required to fill the following:

*Author Name (Required)

*Description

*Image (Which you'll select and upload the image's file from your system and you can also image if you don't like to change to another or leave image)

*Create Page

*Cancel

You'll click Create Page after filling the information or choose to cancel
Please Note: W e have just talked about the left hand side of the Kindle Create App you are getting used to in working with. You must and should note that everything you do on the left is dictated by the right hand side/page of the manuscript displayed on your screen which you are also working on.

Let's quickly have an overview: You can see print settings, theme, save, preview and publish at the right hand side. And view, undo, redo, find and insert on the right hand side. You'll be using/needing all these to create your E-Book.

In the print settings, you'll set how you want your headings, interior et cetera to appear. But it comes after you have done the preliminaries.

In the Theme, you can choose Modern, Classic, Cosmos, or Amour style. The default is usually put in is Modern. You can leave it at that or choose another. For me, I prefer the Modern style because I don't like to adopt old things.

The Save menu, allows you to save your works just like the normal saving by you do on MS Word or other similar application.

The Preview enables you to check and see well how your work has been created and designed before you can publish on Amazon as your ready E-Book.

When you click the Publish button, it'll save it as kpf (that's the code it'll use) and put in front of the original manuscript you started with and save it where you save the same. It will appear as a brown-like format in that file.

Now, for the Body section of your manuscript, you'll be able to use the left hand side very well to create a very beautiful Body/Content. You must know and understand the following well if you want6 to achieve this:

*Chapter Title

*Chapter Subtittle

*Chapter First Paragragh
*Sub heading

*Block Quotes

*Poem

*Separator

*Opening Quotes

*Opening Quote Credit

As said earlier, everything you do in the left hand side is dedicated/controlled by the right hand side but it works with the cursor.

For example; if you want to identify any part of the heading as a chapter, you'll just put your cursor in front of the title and click CHAPTER TITLE. There and then, it identify that part of a heading as a chapter. Similarly, if there is a Chapter Subtitle, you'll do it in the like manner but here, you'll click the Chapter Subtitle.

Another interesting feature in the Kindle Create App is the Chapter First Paragraph which beautifies and makes any part you identify as a beginning First Paragraph of any chapter(s) of your manuscript. All these you can't achieve in the Basic Training part of this knowledge acquisition.

Then you'll design and create the chapters of your manuscript in a similar. If you've been able to achieve this well, you'll have different subheadings at the body section part of your left hand.

Having done that, to get your table of contents, you'll either use the earlier method as pointed out by editing or accepting the table of contents prepared automatically by the Kindle Create App, or you go to insert indicated by + at the top left hand side of your manuscript. But what you'll do is to move onto the beginning of your book. Then you'll go to your first chapter and click to identify where the table of contents should start.

After that, select the table of contents out of the other four subsets of the insert button. This will give you an overview of all you've selected. And after that, click on insert; it'll just create for you a table of contents automatically which becomes part of your that you're formatting.

By now, you would have come up with a beautiful manuscript which I would rather call a ready-made book. If you aren't satisfied with your book yet, you are can still design and edit further. But if you're okay with it, you could save and preview your work. After that, you could proceed to publish.

When you click the publish button to publish, it'll take you to the portion of your computer where you saved the original document you worked with as your manuscript.

Please Note: Here, you're to note that the name of the original document you started with is the same you will come up after all the works you have done on your manuscript, except that it'll show as a light brown or grey colour with kpf in front of the file name. This is what you'll upload on the Amazon site as your E-Book to be endorsed and published.

You just only have to click save now to save and store the beautiful book you've come up with, and you can easily upload on your personal KDP account for publication.

The above is what you can achieve with the well designed Kindle Create App which is not achievable with the Create Space App that you learnt and were taught at the Basic Level Training of this program.

I believe, by now, you're a Master Creator and Designer of an E-Book on Amazon. Therefore, go live your dream of self-publishing! Start publishing your book yourself on Amazon with no money or sponsor or publisher hitches. Start publishing your books right now on Amazon!

SIGNING UP ON AMAZON

It's time we get to knowing how to sign up on Amazon. But first, we have to be acquainted with KDP.

So what's KDP? KDP is Kindle Direct Publishing and it's the first thing we have to do before going to publishing our books. It's actually creating your account on the Amazon platform.

Other Alternative

This is to inform us that if you have account with Payoneer you can use it as another option from cheques.

For those that would like to get paid using their bank account, there is a company that enables you accept payment from US, UK or other countries. It's called Payoneer.

It's completely free to create an account with them.

The first thing you want to do is create an account. Payoneer helps you receive payment via Wire Transfer.

They will give you a bank account which you will enter on Amazon.

Another alternative is that you can make use of an account of someone in the US you trust, for the purpose of your use. However, this is not advisable unless you trust the person concerned very well.

To get your postal code, you may google it- ie your local government postal code.

If You Do Not Have An Account Already With Amazon, You Will Need To Sign Up

When you sign up, you will be sent your OTP. It could be either through your phone number or your email address. As soon as you receive the OTP, immediately input the six digit number into the space provided and you will be granted access. You will then need to wait for further instructions.

Be careful of everything you are filling or clicking. Make sure the information is correct. It is important you fill in your details well because its the same information that will be used to process your checks.

Go to your account and fill up the information. Click and answer one after the other. Ensure your address is correct. Please put address they can reach you with.

Choose Amazon.com which pays in dollars, not UK or other countries. The good news is it will give you information on what they expect and other options.

Please note: You cannot use your phone to publish. It is best you make use of a laptop because of some features you will not easily find accessible in your mobile phone. Use your laptop or a desktop.

STEP BY STEP OF ACCOUNT CREATION

*Type Kdp.amazon.com on your browser

*Log on the prompt screen

*If you have created the account, go to sign in that is a straight forward process

*For those that have account with Amazon you click sign in direct

*Click the Kdp account and start the process of creating the Kdp account for those without Amazon account.

a. Your Name

b. Email

c. Password

d. Re-enter password

*After filling the up spaces you can now click your Kdp account.

*It would ask for authentication

*A message (OTP) would be sent to your email

*Copy the number

*Paste or type it.

*Revalidate your account

*Click again.

The second stage of Account Creation:

Log on to your account

a.Tax Information

b. Bank information

c. Type in **10012(if in Nigeria)
d. Getting paid, Ignore it

Tax Information:

a. Take Interview

b. Unclick the Tin

B. Click "The country you are does not issue Tin (This for Nigerians) Not for US or UK citizens".

e. Continue

f. Sign ...... Put your full name

g. Go through the preview

h. Click and Submit form

I. Exit Interview

Please Note:

The basic requirement for publishing your eBook is formatting. There are two ways you can format your eBook :
*Manual with MS word

Using kindle create space template.

For the tax information especially on TIN, people should just click on 'My country does not provide a TIN". Click on the non-US citizen option and other options including, my country doesn't provide Tin numbers... will pop up

FINAL STEP: PUBLISHING YOUR EBOOK ON KDP

I must congratulate you for having come this far. You've done a great job. Thumbs up to you.

Now for the final stage, you're expected to finish by publishing your ebook on kdp (kindle direct publishing.

*Please Note: Here you're going to be redirected to another page. Nothing concerns you to click except kdp. To get the next line of action to do, please consider and follow the following steps:

*Under create a new title click kindle ebook

* If you are there start filling the form

*Book Title

*Subtitle, if your book has it

*Next if it is going to be series, you write 1 but if not, ignore

*NEXT EDITION 1 Or First

*FILL YOUR FULL NAME

*CONTRIBUTOR- IGNORE

PRIMARY AUTHOR--- YES

* NEXT

*DESCRIPTION OF THE BOOK

*ABOUT THE BOOK: Copy and paste it. You should have written and saved it before now.

*CLICK I OWN THE COPY

*NEXT PUBLISHING RIGHT
*NEXT YOUR WORDS TO DESCRIBE THE BOOK MINIMUM 5

*It could be key words or phrases

*Categories. Click nonfiction

*Then click motivational and inspirational

*Then click SELF HELP

*Then go up and CLICK General

*Leave Children

*US grand range leave it

*Pre order. Already click for you

Save and continue

Note: Ebook Does Not Need Isbn

Please don't touch paperback for now, you will complicate things for yourself. But if you have mastered the art of designing you could try out your skills in using the various images available in the Amazon gallery to create and design your papaerbacks or you could upload already designed or created image on your system to make your paperback.

You can then save and continue and proceed to launching and publishing your eBook which would pass through review by the Amazon group and could come out live and direct to be published in 72 hours (3 days) if it meets all the necessary requirements.

ACKNOWLEDGEMENT

I thank Pastor Mrs. Olufunke who happens to be one of the organizers of GoGlobal Publishing Free EBook, a platform on WhatsApp wherein we partakers were taught how to publish our works on Amazon for free in the Basic Class. I equally thank Mr Eshiebor Simon. I duly acknowledge and pay homage to the mastermind and brain behind the awesome Write for me Organization, Arc Solomon Okpa Etchie, the Ogapatapata himself, and the other organizers who were support him in making the Organization move forward. May God continue to bless you, your family and everything that concern you sir. Thank you so much for this wonderful opportunity to learn and earn this digital knowledge from you.

ABOUT THE AUTHOR

Ibrahim O. Arasi

The author is a gentle and an easy-going person who writes stories and poems. He studied mechanical engineering in the University of Ilorin and he is a building engineering contractor.

Besides being a short-story writer and poet, he is a motivational writer and some of his books (apart from this one) are soon to be published on Amazon.